Gifted Wares

Playwright by

Baruch Menache

New York, NY
United States of America

Published by McWest & Associates
 ISBN: 978-1-971928-40-1

<u>**Setting**</u>

The play moves across two timelines:

The present day, and ten years earlier.

Locations shift between bedrooms, ports, bars, side streets, stables, therapy offices, and storm-lit nights.

<u>On Language</u>

The dialogue is intentionally stylized. It blends poetic rhythm, rural cadence, biblical undertone, and modern disarray.

Note: This work contains themes of sexual violence, incest, and psychological trauma.

Act 1: The Girls' Secrets
[Present day]

[Scene: A dimly lit hotel room, two girls sit in quiet conversation, their words hanging in the air like the weight of untold secrets. The atmosphere is heavy, filled with the tension of what's unsaid, men had been over and had left.]

DAUGHTER:

> Come sister, tell the tale of youth,
>
> Hasn't a boy in sight
>
> Given charm to patented film;
>
> Lime yellowed with adornment?
>
> Plastering shades
>
> Seem to garner at sunrise;
>
> Moon only but lingers.
>
> Keep us asleep—they too may be awake.
>
> Will they come back, to retreat the shame?

STEPDAUGHTER:

> Oh, there's not a worry in sight
>
> Of shining lights to the everbright.
>
> Yesterday was its last
>
> Two days were its delight
>
> And the final days' come
>
> Devoid of a boyish respite.

WAITRESS:

> To disturb a kiss
> In their leisure,
> Address is my duty
> Of fulfilled perchance.
> The accused make service tenable,
> Given choice-maker his allotment.
> Servile banking without a receipt,
> Beveled goods despisin' human form.
>
> Breakfast served, madam.
> Fried, skilled with a honey glaze
> Buttered to afternoon, oil'd to Friday morn.

[They ignore the server and breakfast, rolling their eyes.]

DAUGHTER:

> Confirmed? They seem suspect for a few.
> Arisen at nine, betwixt in graces' mess.
>
> Eye you, is that a hologram
> Taken a liking to a halo,
> Fixed a sure way out.

STEPDAUGHTER:

> It will be confirmed when I see it wash away,
> Till then we ado the secrecy of youth.
>
> Aroma takes favor to flavor,
> Secrecy—better with eggs,
> Rouses spirits to the comforting fine.

DAUGHTER:

> Fine by me, tell me your way,
> I may conjure but not deny.
> Take heed of every word, none to avail.
> Find me when short-of-change;
> Scratchy pockets and dimmed dimes.
>
> Whenever we turn,
> 'tis the page of its aftermath.

STEPDAUGHTER:

    Don't you say—at lat'est a-day,

    Went his name, tried in time.

    Croaked, void of laugh;

    Name for weakened knees,

    Foothold with meager whims

    Everlasting of the arrow

    Seeking resolute to the bow,

    With a winter harvest

    To a farmers' lien.

DAUGHTER:

    Oh, do tell, avenge, purge that spirit!

    Don't conceal the implied fate.

    Peace'd by the merry shroud,

    Dost done do the deed twice now

    Once in bed and once again.

    So do not spare a detail or two,

    Repeated for the everyday;

    Cross-examined—court's ruling

    Charged the fellow for sinisters' aim.

    Spitballed to adjoiner a-year,

    Try me for pink in whatever the fate,

Will do in blanket spate.
Send for mercenaries, harken folk;
Blood is mercy if power gets her day.
Stark the night with simple folk;
Mused immortality.

STEPDAUGHTER:

Frightened of peril's close
Just in the same afar.
Contorting namesake,
Fostering rebellions,
Witnesses—we are.

Shadowed hands, halved a whole
Crowded over smiles—trying times.
Say, the off-putting mentor,
Correct the incorrect!
Do this, do that,
Don't do it all,
Do none for a fall.
That song of tears,
Despairin' farewell.

[Enter two friends from the other room]

IRRITATING FRIEND:

> To seem a shine—colorless—
>
> Without selection, tuning away.
>
> Out, trusting the Sun with a glare.
>
> Wherever you may go
>
> I'll double in step,
>
> Unless a ring brings to a sing.

BACKUP FRIEND:

> Quiet! Adulted minds speak languages afar,
>
> 'Tis when we silence to believe a faint.
>
> Get on with your duty!

IRRITATING FRIEND:

> Come, sleep is a fighting grievance,
>
> Do away from that.
>
> A will which repeats for the kill.

[The two friends fall back asleep on couch, the server leaves with suspect]

STEPDAUGHTER:

>Strayed along lines of sandilions,
>Send me to the backchannel
>Who'd look swayed or forward.
>Believed, sustained trade-winds,
>Truckers in bearing, me in toad;
>Rest-assured sanity.

>Girl made from straw
>Him from meat.
>Fire stoked and mocked
>Envy encased in touring tests.

[Serious tone]

>Tented storms and drained sewage,
>Named in time, so I'll tell you again,
>Shambled we will be—all over this.

DAUGHTER:

>Cared' away our soul,
>As 'plain'd as we might.
>This night and the next
>Will be sat in silence.

>The third will do the deed.
>Trust the merit

That gives weight to words.

A rainbow tells us so

In color coded perfection;

For now, coolness of shores.

Will be found too fraught in bondage chill,

Lather me in cloth and comfort;

A redemption from premeditative horror.

STEPDAUGHTER:

Training wheels give moons' flight

Fighters supposed in lost ground.

Alas to cry out, 'alas',

To decide mine-awful fate,

Destiny dare not return in gold,

Signage for a passenger

Marked a redden hue.

Act 2: The Father's Dark Past
[Ten years earlier]

[Scene: In her bedroom]

FATHER:

> Shine for me dearest being,
>
> Cover your spell
>
> Trusting proudness from me.

DAUGHTER:

> Oh, if that is all I want;
>
> Enough will never be.
>
> Do you now—cry me a flow—as promised?

STEPDAUGHTER:

> Pledged I am to see this through.

FATHER:

> Show me your girth,
>
> Mother and daughter,
>
> Cloth liv'est as Bible fold,
>
> Sheets of lament and eager foil
>
> Did give ruin to mine-oiled name.
>
> Corruptin' was given a—a chance,
>
> Blackened by such coal—this is my resolute!

INVISIBLE GOODMAN:

> You don't say, sire!

To lay with thy kind, treatise older than wheat.

First wine clothed from nakedness.

FATHER:

Kind you with words, the bosom of ideas,

Merit the excuse in a cleaned heart.

Resting soul is bandwidth to body;

Arm to foot, canopy probing rainfall

To pluck the first of my loss.

INVISIBLE GOODMAN:

How thoughtlessness disguise merriment?

Flesh falls to disfavor in an ounce;

A pound speedily in such an act.

Gone is any return,

Pleasure squatter than mackerel in shark's tooth.

[As father complacent mumble, stepdaughter talks to daughter]

STEPDAUGHTER:

> Shooken' by a steal'd encounter,
>
> Water reservoir'd seem waned.
>
> Countering with stealth friends,
>
> Fearing rebellions—cursed then.
>
> Unknown is spirit that chases
>
> Better than a find—always.

[Exit stepdaughter, sympathetic glance]

FATHER:

> Cured to give abode to father's father
>
> That may offer a grave-rose.
>
> Any furtherment be amended
>
> Same as different chills the icebox.
>
> Apologetic as mannerism,
>
> Pity robed purple hue
>
> Upon chairs burned for confrontation.

INVISIBLE HENCHMEN:

> Kill 'em sirs, kill 'em if it makes ya happy!
>
> Right the wrong, justice-clock set by the hour.
>
> Minutes, seconds—circle too fast;
>
> Determined for the hard lock.

FATHER:

> Trust seems favor that loyalty deems shamed.
>
> T'where is the end of lewdness, running afar—a cry,
>
> Tears that never cover the deed—spoiled water.
>
> Can't this be gone from mind?
>
> A return for which there is none.

INVISIBLE HENCHMEN:

> Ha, you give line-of-credit to your deeds
>
> Eyes do no gander on this night;
>
> Fright in no service or paid for.
>
> Pleasure had no end to either tail,
>
> Grab 'n go, packaged for forgetfulness.
>
> Memory is a picture, film for those un-livid.
>
> Chanced upon occasion as your rite of passage.

INVISIBLE GOODMAN:

> Who dost understand the ways of plenty?
>
> In arrows had their mead, with stealth their brew.
>
> Shunned at the merriment of being
>
> That favors a story and its tale.
>
> Evermore is repealing sights,

Taken from a maiden's bed.

Reprimanding for sheathed salvation,

Cursed at the plate, cued for dining.

Founded in axe, molded in flackery.

All of life for none but thyself.

INVISIBLE HENCHMEN:

Sure, by and by, made a few coins

To fit the average pocket, some extra to chime.

Shown at once—

Scavenger of momentous greed,

Insatiable at the brim of expectation.

Listenin' 'n grace made well to escape,

Dolly of a trolly to a real world.

Hardened to its face, destined is to be born.

Do you speak of that, such like that?

To live the burden of birth, resolved not ever yonder?

[Quiet to herself]

DAUGHTER:

> Delirious eyes finds its maker
> Words, unaffectionate to sloppy lips.
> Salvia satiates a food of merriment,
> Nothing second to that.

[Father leaves bashfully]

Act 3: Father's Walk
[Ten years earlier—weeks before the deed]

[Scene: Father, after working at the port as a day-laborer, he returns and muses to himself on his walk home]

FATHER:

> Ha! Sailors' dress conforms to sea,
>
> Ocean swells to the sky wells.
>
> Disfavor at the race for color,
>
> As image covers image, reckon I do the same.

[Stumbled over a pothole]

> The ape and t-rex do their damage,
>
> Functioning a climb or silver tooth.
>
> The spear is found in each living thing,
>
> Expected man to give up arms or alms,
>
> Lays the bed of willing or—so.
>
> Animated weapon, courage to her resting place,
>
> Axed Viking is the succumbed bosom.
>
> The bayonet for English foe is mine virgin,
>
> Shunned, no different than a hated triumph.
>
> Trophy allotted to indifferent men;
>
> A trait that knows thy vison.
>
> Praises given to the Saint,
>
> Sons and daughters shan't behold legacy.

Glory pasted in rewritten books—a legion
of Marcus
Cared the silver coin, chanced to be citizen.

[Overhearing some of his mumble]

HOMELESS MAN:

> Time tingles with error, long after a victory sweep,
>
> Away the epoch to rediscover; Egypt and its pearls.
>
> Thrown a youngling, in his growth a loathing Pharaoh.
>
> Mystique—the justifiable mind do the mighty wicked
>
> A fool's most gravitatin' slump will not succumb.

FATHER:

> Wayward soul to give bodily advice,
>
> Must the guilt pang to reveal the indiscreet?
>
> Have I ridden the slope, detest 'n detest?
>
> Anguished presence, solemn of misdirection,
>
> Sense from the insensible, dust-bowl to a derby.

HOMELESS MAN:

> Sandy dunes dug to the bay
>
> Parched eyes eager for watery slopes.
>
> Encampment is the soldier's day
>
> The war of three-n-twenty minutes;
>
> Act of moment is frail and gone in't the next.

FATHER:

> Sentiment endows itself through mist
>
> Covering fate with sparkles.
>
> And she—she—perfumes,
>
> Covering late,
>
> Teeth broached 'n classical gratuity.

[A flicker of something—regret, maybe.]

> At last said: I did good. I did good!
>
> But I—
>
> I'm fallen.
>
> Errs have beaten this heart too.
>
> Soon—the alarm will sound.

[Silence. He looks off.]

> And with mail over the tree
>
> Yes—
>
> To the cave of agitation.

Act 4: Work & Carrousel
[Present-day]

[Scene: On their way to work]

STEPDAUGHTER:

> Backseat for the stage play,
> Rowed by the class of seekers,
> Runnage from pained superstition.
> Grandmothers presupposin',
> Offered a marking 'n hand.

DAUGHTER:

> Introducin' weather to a faceless frown,
> Satisfaction to keep will at bay,
> A shore to a sailor lost at sea,
> Oceanless of bottomed trouble.

> Thoughts arrivin' a-second too late,
> Aspired evil destined to show;
> Lax on buttons and levers.

> Arguing sense is a rebellion,
> Given to the extra citation.
> Swayed from muscled strength
> Tool-less ape with a marking grin
> Burdened of organic function.

[Work hard for half the day, take leave together, with smart friend]

[At the carrousel, later in the afternoon]

STEPDAUGHTER:

> Here we are!

DAUGHTER:

> Shan't we do different this season?

STEPDAUGHTER:

> Never–girl, this is our time!

DAUGHTER:

> Time for what?

STEPDAUGHTER:

> Nothing—the maker of wombs
> Without words to complicate,
> Speeches, injury to open ears.

SMART FRIEND:

> Competition as a manner of folk,
> Destroyed in the founding stones;
> Grayed right out th' blue sky.
>
> Friendship to vile the otherwise,
> Allegiances in refuge of hate,
> Bonds to be less than alone.
> Sanctity is never called her name,

A billow sends favor to a rock
All that comes together dissolves in skin.

Fetch the good one, in solitude shines;
Friendships to adorn, allegiances to merry;
Bonds instill love in its dearth.
Fancy a reconciliation?

STEPDAUGHTER:

Memories dost give me right
I was there, wasn't I!
Gladness will be over,
Giddy' up little horse
'round the city we go.
Ha! Ha! Ha!

DAUGHTER:

As dreams hasten' move mountains,
If valleys we reside it 'be our choosin'.

Get a figure on them
To count my coins.
Might be worth the chatter
Ablemen turn ape over its *chang*.

Spirit—my soul unawaken that I enjoy the cave,

Tell town of my insolence lest they fare enjoyment

Tell makers of dirt that skirts resemble womanhood.

Tell them, lest they envy the freedom of this carrousel;

That they have found a resting place—

Wayward from me.

SMART FRIEND:

Give the lion its meat,

The tiger his share,

The fox a keen eye

And a meager man his laugh.

DAUGHTER:

Retribution! Ha!

To apologize is to forgive

To return is to be,

To be born is to have lived.

Grandeur in faith of humility,

Delighted to show its hour

When the hourglass empties its sand

Without elderly folk to turn it over.

Say it ain't so, that I'll live the shoulder

Of islands that give nothing 'n take even less.

Be gone to my journey to learn mistakes.

Till then,

Be the drippings of milk from mothers'
breast,

When suckling was free

And the neighboring child found no envy in
my fill.

SMART FRIEND:

Grandness without a maker.

DAUGHTER:

Sundry laundry of garlic smells.

Small is a clovered mind;

Dreams that haven't flight.

Color, faded before dried

Is never a speech by the merry.

[Rowdy crowd passes, they lose coherence]

STEPDAUGHTER:

Dandiness is fee'd expense

Dateless calendar, timeless clock

Numbers reversed its counting.

Lack! Ducklings ponderin' the swaddle,

Chicklings on soft grass.

Despisin' the old man

Who eats more than his share.
Haven't you a crow to steer you right?

Act 5: Stable Boy
[Present-day]

[Scene: Daughter with friend taking horse lessons, now with Stable Boy as they ride horses.]

STABLE BOY:

> Hissed to a turnaround stable boy,
>
> Showed him your looks;
>
> Love drapes all rebellion.
>
> Mocks the saddle we ride
>
> Missed a step of the showman.
>
> At-last she sits at my step,
>
> On fertile ground rides;
>
> Makeshift of a romance.

DAUGHTER:

> Asked and answered,
>
> To profession thy betray
>
> As a maiden on its back.

STABLE BOY:

> Horses saddled to lady's comfort
>
> Sunlight is to be sunset,
>
> Do you take me as I am?

DAUGHTER:

> In the parched grass, attending.
>
> Ha, Willoughby was here before, wasn't he?

STABLE BOY:

> The last fortnight.

DAUGHTER:

> Sure must've been a ride
> Browned leather is my choice of love
> Sailors at ports for a lifetime of sail;
> Card games take them overly joyous.
>
> Grander is a heart that splits in two,
> For the right arm and the left,
> To hold during crisis and love
> With equal footing.

STABLE BOY:

> I take console in your speech,
> Words do injury but never perjury,
> Round the bend is back to the shacks
> Where thy pretty girls wash saying prayer.
>
> Bye now, bye.

DAUGHTER:

> Until we meet again.

[Her friend, aside.]

DAUGHTER'S FRIEND:

> Tell me fellow hasn't the eye,
>
> Doesn't give quite the mellow,
>
> To discuss the next meeting
>
> Taking place on firm ground.

DAUGHTER:

> Come now, don't make peasant humor.

[Daughter and friend depart]

[Enter two friends of stable boy.]

FRIEND 1:

> Backdoor'd the stage,
>
> To stand upper'd;
>
> Staged a hall-pass.
>
> Friendship lingered passed prime,
>
> Fellowship lead the hardy-way,
>
> Family for the finish line.
>
> Bread baked in croissants,
>
> Meat in a delicatessen,
>
> Oils with devoted fats.
>
> Smoother than the slick,
>
> Both never do the trick.

FRIEND 2:

> They have entered the exit door
> And never glanc'd the difference
> Nor given denial some plausibility.

STABLE BOY:

> Station your jewels in thieves' delight
> Let the rich go to heaven,
> 'n aquamarine to speak of oceans.
> For it is oceans we need talk
> And blood replaced of the ruby,
> Earnest to a cutthroat diamond.
> The robe of cheap purple
> Gave door to the amethyst;
> The lazuli prides green for nature.
>
> Keep the wallet that holds promise
> When bargain lost the edge in line-not-to-cross
> And the fun is unfound from business Joe
> Who thinks starvation is 'round the bend
> And eats the game after the lion.

FRIEND 1:

> Take another lap,
> Try that dice at the table of men
> Who sleep unscheduled.

Dare make a fool 'n twice the arrangement,
Fencing dignity to pay amends out of value.

FRIEND 2:

Softing Friday do away sense,
Nor late Sunday that gives some back.

STABLE BOY:

Sayonara!
This was a party of two!

[Exit all, but stable boy]

[Caressing a horse, he mumbles with an overture]

STABLE BOY:

Styled a fashion to a Shakespearean love;
Demise remov'd, tranquil dilute,
Granulated comfort trounced the opportune.
Cavern of old, wine in spirits,
Raised man-cattle, red-blushed of failed love,
Green of ventured stray.

Love never free,
Scrupled to the wisher
At portside held,
Coupled apart.

Act 6: Father's Friend
[Ten years earlier—weeks before the deed]

[Scene: Working at the port]

FATHER'S FRIEND:

> Shadows forming in circle tones,
>
> Glimpsing a flamingo in flight.
>
> Reach the approachable
>
> Angering the rebellious son
>
> Who just loves the idea
>
> More so than father.

FATHER:

> Dined in theory
>
> Eaten with fairy,
>
> Sat alongside pain,
>
> Canvassed for an entranceway.

FATHER'S FRIEND:

> Subtle forms the angelic spear;
>
> Marksman, a lonesome raising,
>
> Whiteness to a blackened scope.
>
> Tales of wrenching corsets,
>
> Groomed to the expectin' trait.
>
> Damn beauty!
>
> Salvation is farther back.

INVISIBLE HENCHMEN:
Resilience marks change
Mystery does the trick
That never finds in due time.

Fencing for a fact,
Depositing a way-around.
Gave mother proudness,
Father a steel-toe reluctance
To bring shame to faces,
Disillusioned to the inquirers.
If only to say: "I have done it
And you cannot understand."

Said more than allotted
If it was revenge—
I would have known it;
Mediation found
In a princess's style.

A crown of jewels,
Imperfect stone and rock;
Stubborn in place
Fastened by pasted glue
From kindergarten shares.

So we make fun of the fact
That we can make fun.
With a harrowing left
'til understanding
Succeeds nimble minds.

FATHER:

Veilin' deeds in the scope
Dallydaises in winter sun
That hopes for a 'morrow
Better than yesterday.

Act 7: Stepdaughter at Bar
[Present-day]

[Scene: Stepdaughter drunk at a local bar, talking to the bartender]

STEPDAUGHTER:

> Dancing prey
>
> Legs make right;
>
> Mouthing words,
>
> Slips of tongue.

BARTENDER:

> Shadowy songs in a choir,
>
> A party in the fortnight,
>
> On to the next.

STEPDAUGHTER:

> To shake the spirits from anklets,
>
> Crowned from an everlastin' dream,
>
> To awaken would cause a cry—a stir.
>
> Shallow markers preferred Sunday evenin'
>
> As goes radio silence of future trouble.
>
> Born to give favor, offering is what I do.

[They sleep together]

[After intercourse]

[Silently to herself]

STEPDAUGHTER:

> Charged I am, given pleasure to the drum;
> It'd sync and never marry,
> To wash the humble stay.

[Fingers shaking]

> Fingers trembling!
> No dear,
> Body! Have you no shame
> To give rest?

[Hallucinates father]

> Oh jitter—my father,
> Go inside your own.
> Nimble mice, you!
> Go into your hold.

> Leave to my defenses;
> A disrupt befall
> As pleasure had its filling
> To take a breath of peace,
> Adjourned at tinglings request.

> No dear, your confinement will end,
> Soon enough, you hear!
> A toil, I alone will bear,
> Stay, stay now—in your youthful slumber.

[Out loud, bartender]

BARTENDER:

My dear, what were you saying?

[She turns the other way, rolls eyes]

Act 8: Night Before

[Ten years earlier—the night before the deed]

[Scene: Dim light. A faint storm outside, lying in bed in heat soak]

FATHER:

> Joined as one abode a frightened kiss
>
> Reddened by passion
>
> Mixed with a clever mind
>
> Saddened by a note of heard music.
>
>
> Doesn't a night give rest
>
> To a charmed daybreak?
>
> Quell me to an imprisonment.
>
> Shan't a mind be a revenger?
>
> Sifted coal on babes' tongue.

[Rain begins to pour, screaming out loud to no one.]

> Shutters keep rain at bay
>
> Shan't you be a fool to all?
>
> Slower to service,
>
> Remedy to adult crops;
>
> A wailing' farmer's last hope.
>
>
> Rain! Vile! On soaky heat.

Act 9: Before the Deed
[Ten years earlier—the day before the deed]

[Scene: Upon getting wind of father's intentions]

DAUGHTER:

> Smiled to a foreboding memory,
> Trusted the senses 'n gave more;
> More than asked for a handle.
> Synopsis had a trail of earthenware
> Gouged the air dost soften in attire.
>
> T'were does the effect of daybreak
> In evenin' starlight—a navigator's bliss.
> Waters calm in a warn'd forecast;
> Storm await a merry day.

STEPDAUGHTER:

> Doesn't favor turn a tide?
> A reservoir extend furthermore.
> To flood the town by its devices,
> To protect a womb by its charm.

DAUGHTER:

> Where I go none returns.
> That laid girl of David's chair;
> Distressed maid to princess disgrace,
> Brother unveiled, bridal surreal'd.

Hate and love—a token
Arivin' the same island shore
Aback the Albatross at sea

Say no more, words fail the lips
Regret to faint the survivor.
Willed the creature by creation,
Dost settle a land taught ages prior.

Fence the gate serene,
At your command I see bygone.
Guilt creeps the legs of despair
Where love has found its maker.
The deed of punishment outlived pain,
Canvassing the abyss to paint astray,
Never the same, never different.
Say a prayer, words by a few,
Silence apt the wayback.
In trial, the err are found
And all is erred when so is sought.
Away from me you go,
Never your face in this light!

STEPDAUGHTER:

Sharp words told in demise,

Hope thought to heal
To revenge the spirit,
And know the good from not-so.
That a sister to be;
In whatever way—unforeseen.

[Tears]

DAUGHTER:

Bye now, ado to the lost sprit of Rome,
To the princess of David—dethroned.

Act 10: The Deed
[Ten years earlier]

FATHER:

> Centerpiece laid affront
>
> Waving a spell, a witches' tale.
>
> Clothed in secrecy, girded with scent
>
> Spilled with lusting talk—
>
> I can undo the tale.

DAUGHTER:

> Stammering a speech,
>
> Action at better-a-will.
>
> Time gave no peace,
>
> Action to make resolute.

[He lay with her]

[To herself she mumbles]

DAUGHTER:

> To a slumbering foil
>
> Crafted a scribe.
>
> Dictate the terms,
>
> Blood on pages—seal'd.

> Feather'd as a bird's story
>
> Wielding power in hands' sensation,
>
> Let the mind astray 'til deeds are done.

[He finishes]

Act 11: Therapy
[Present-day]

DAUGHTER:

Consumption barred contestation

Troubling the talk of decision.

[Wise man passing the window overhears the discourse]

THERAPIST:

Made in dark places across glaring light,

Someday placed in its puzzle hole—someday,

Black until white, missing 'til found.

Sorrow is but delight uncovered from dusted pursuits,

Sharing a melody but on off-putting ground.

Sampled an Eden reserve, t'were a child trespass.

Finding father at the helm of desperation,

Mother at the well of reflection,

Decided a fate of ten years.

DAUGHTER:

Pa told me, didn't I listen.

Whatever the way, together is a'molded frame.

Be it the painting of artists' pain,

The scolded dish to a chef's entrée;
Forgotten soul to the remembered name.
Why is luxury of the soul,
Reminisce in future, save for details.

THERAPIST:

Coming away to find a circle,
Squared at the face of corners;
Only for the three-pronged cluster.
Front in back, center to the left;
Then again—at your six.

DAUGHTER:

Desperation to tell face
Delighting an urge
Repeated a quelled flare-up;
Until the next meeting
Timed and placed.

[Last remark before she leaves the office]

THERAPIST:

Fancy a woodpecker in the season of love,
Backdrop to a runaway girl.
She says more than she is—never the right
tale.

Sanity in a private love

That made public the activity.
Stay a while. Stay and forget evermore
love—
Eccentric dreams funneled in credence
Giving life a final hoorah,
Sensitive to the cradle.

[A pause, a final call.]

Shine a silver bullet,
Cached in the wrinkle.

[Wise man continues, chanced upon a tree, with reverence]

THE WISE MAN:

> Deeds, oh deeds, they set me free.
>
> Trees, oh trees, they say, "fine by me."

[Steps forward, eyes upward]

> Has trust forgotten the begetter?
>
> In a spell of moments that sought rest,
>
> Someday, when trees speak, they'll say:
>
> "Why are you listening when rumbled leaves devour autumns' soundscape?"

[Turns, gesturing to the earth]

> For erectous Mother Earth
>
> Cried tears dried from a burial shroud.
>
> Fancy a thought that has no ground.
>
> Fable is now spoken in mnemonic sequence,
>
> Stories grandfathered taste of despised desert.
>
> Beholden to a Greek conqueror with Anthony envy,
>
> Saturnine to the fellowship of cattle—mooring lands,
>
> Finds taste in blade-grass and sensibility in a shepherd.
>
> Let them twist 'n turn, I say, lest a daughter get her milks filling.

Love never comes until it does
And gone before a better grip.
When a troubled heart meets an infinite mass
Where waves disrupt vessels of sea
Departing to its aim and direction.
For once the way back is shorter, more clear,
How can love be grounded in fire?
Whence does the feather float in the storm?

Act 12: Father Regret
[Ten years earlier—six months after deed]

[Scene: Talking to the maid]

FATHER:

> Gift wrapping a Childs' dream
>
> Ending is the exchange of bodies.
>
> Finalized in the great betrayal
>
> That healing will not satirize
>
> Nor the gift of mind.
>
> Sensuality will give respite
>
> Of playful final games.
>
> Thrown a towel at thy maker,
>
> Sunsets that do no illumination,
>
> Disgust finds—fiend.

MAID:

> To the gift on high, ribbon bowed.
>
> Mothers' tell of love,
>
> Colorless as space 'n time.
>
> Attempted to circle a square,
>
> Trembling the rupture,
>
> Remembering the silence.

FATHER:

> Sorrow proceeds the inevitable,
>
> Chosen hindsight of a known void;

Awake at last with no memory to unfold.

Salvation to the choiced road
Where East blows mighty,
Where goes the trenched gift.

[Maid seems suspect]

FATHER:

Come back at nine I'll see you paid,
The hassle of my beholdance.

Act 13: Confrontation
[Present-day]

[Scene: Staring at the mirror in disgust before the act]

DAUGHTER:

> The reflective surface gives chills,
> Shining away misfortune of words.
> Weirded the momentous tone
> That stole an extra glance.
> Hadn't graciousness told of one?
>
> And it was this, this—-that the mirror lied,
> Lies that had kingdoms wrapped in blankets
> And scrawny men devis'd in devilish pillows.
>
> Call the glass maker for his return,
> Expect a refund
> For goods disserviced the benefactor,
> Now, let nighttime give us rest.

[Enters fathers bedroom, kills him][After, she speaks upon him]

DAUGHTER:

> Do you, pa, do you love me?
> Well—
> Servant to public trades,

Love—
You must love me.
How could you not?
There, by my correction,
Beckoning my perfection,
It must be there;
We will dig
Until we find it.

Mustn't get in the way,
Telling lies?
Quiet, you—
Because you love me.
Quiet now.
Don't speak
To quell the love.
I am sure now,
Evermore,
That you can't find a way
Away from my love.

Surely it is you
Who bend knees for me.
Stop the smile—
It may

Remove
Some love.
To hate—
So we can unearth a potion.
(You guessed it.)
Love.

Get on with it.
Just say it:
You love me!

I hate you.
Always have
Even in a sky's charade,
Go back to the hole.
Hey—
There's dirt to cover yourself.

I do love you
So smile now.

[Enters stepdaughter]

[Stepdaughter staring at her bosom in the mirror, with the daughter on her bed with some blood stains.]

STEPDAUGHTER:

> They came in fast,
> Those flapping wings,
> Butterflies called insects.
>
> My dreary name——-
> Call me mother.
>
> Call me a flapping disgrace,
> Wings sized by volume,
> Caterpillar reeling dust particles.
>
> Trust me for a fall
> I'll trust the demise.
> Gives graciousness a-chance
> Love of the self-appointed princess,
> Translucent like the ember rock.
>
> On a lonely ocean bay,
> Caress between two hills,
> No history to Adam—sorry Pastor.

They sat as an only bird,
Ready to fly a nest-coop
Overtaken by a weasel
Who'd laid out to rest.

From a scorching sun
That did no hurt but shine,
As was destined to do.
A moon readied to give tide
Disrupted the sailor from Morning Prayer—
The pirate from looting a friend's canister.

And so you call the devil its name,
Never will the shadow be your wayside
Bitten through teeth of hunger.

That's the animal that we all are
And will ever be.

-The End-

About the Author

Baruch Menache writes at the intersection of narrative, philosophy, and lyric expression. His work spans poetry, essays, and theatrical pieces that examine the interior life and its many thresholds. He lives in New York with his wife and children.

www.ingramcontent.com/pod-product-compliance
Lightning Source LLC
Chambersburg PA
CBHW051415050726
47595CB00010B/4074